Making Your Own Raw Milk Baby Formula

&

All-Age Nutrient Drinks at Home

Almost Identical to Breast Milk

Baby, Toddler, Big Kid/Teen/Adult Versions

For Baby, Toddler, Teen, Adults, & Elderly

Plant Based Version Included!

Make with Raw Cow, Camel, Goat & Sheep Milks (even Yak, Horse or Water Buffalo milk will do!)

Note to the Reader

This formula recipe is almost identical to breast milk and calls for raw, organic, grass-fed, A-2 Jersey cow milk, and all organic (non GMO) ingredients. Around the world, many other milks can be used (camel, goat, sheep, horse, yak, water buffalo, etc.) What matters is how the animal is treated and how pure and energized the quality of the milk is. Pasteurized milk can be used in an emergency; plant-based milks can also be substituted (homemade is best, as you can control the water quality). All of these would be superior to commercial formulas which contain added unnatural minerals and harmful fillers. Also, please see the tips section of this cookbook for information on the importance of the water quality in this formula.

This recipe is a variation with additions, based on the original posting of Sarah Pope via an online article for the Healthy Home Economist.

Table of Contents

MADE WITH LOVE

Introduction

Did you ever feel helpless, knowing only two options, breast milk or commercial formula? For all of the women who didn't make enough milk or weren't able to breastfeed, busy working moms, C-section moms, and adoptive & foster parents who weren't able to get donor breast milk; to anyone who has ever wanted another way to feed their child something nourishing, chemical free and organic without having to squeeze it from their own body. To give them something as primal and as ancient as the revered and mystical cow, itself! Look no further; there is another way to create a loving concoction of 'just-like-breast milk' formula for your baby, and once they're older, a way to feed them their greens and healthy fats; adults can even drink it; we're never too old for the benefits of raw milk! We all know the longstanding argument of 'breastfed is best' vs. 'fed is best', but I think...Mother Nature is right, "Nourished is Best!"

Dedication & Acknowledgement

NOURISHED IS BEST

To the Great Cosmic Mother, the Holy Sophia: I AM Your Vessel; mold me, use me. I thank the Archangels and angels (especially Michael); my most trusted Ancestors, Ascended Masters, and Spirit Guides (especially Jesus, King David, Anna, Mother Mary, Mary Magdalene, Sarah, Isis, Hathor, Green Tara, Aphrodite, Quan Yin, White Buffalo Woman, and all Keepers of The Light). To the various authors keeping the wisdom of the ages at our fingertips and those breathing new life into the world by teaching the ancient rites and rituals through their beautiful Mystery Schools – I bless your continued and important work.

To my Beloved and Twin Flame, Michael, and our earth angels and gurus, MM & MJ – Everything I do is for you and our sacred bond. May our life of truth and authenticity inspire others to seek the divine within and around them. To our children's Godmother, Maria, who runs the Our Lady of the UniverseShrine in Bronx,NY –without you, our Life would not be complete. To our midwife, Nancy Giglio, who empowers other women to step into their power. For my Earthly mother and twin sister (my 'wombie'), Linda and Cynthia, for always supporting my endeavors. For my soul sister Ada, for Abby, Nicole,Jackie, Christine, and all the long-time friendswho have supportedme and my journey – and to the new group of wonderful and conscious women I've recently met – all working on their beautiful healing journeys and raising their vibrations for the good of humanity. To our relatives and neighbors, your support means the world. And to the soulful and kind people of TAOU Studio in Richmond, Virginia, for giving me a space to come home to my body, my temple, and to realize that IT is my higher self's vehicle for DIVINITY in this world of physical form. May the division in the world cease, and may there be peace in the heartsand minds of all.

Raw Milk Baby Formula

NEWBORN TO 6-9 MONTHS

PREP TIME: 10 MIN
TOTAL TIME: 20 MIN
SERVINGS: APPROX. 80 OZ.

4 Cups Raw Animal Milk of Choice
4 Cups Filtered Mineral Water
8 Tbsp Lactose
4 Tbsp Raw or Pasteurized Cream (optional)*
1 Tbsp Liquid Whey (Raw, Organic) (optional)*
1 Tbsp Cod Liver Oil
0.5 Tbsp Butter Oil
2 Tbsp Sunflower Oil
2 Tbsp Extra Virgin Olive Oil
4 Tbsp Virgin Coconut Oil
4 Tbsp Nutritional Yeast
4 Tbsp Gelatin
0.5 Tbsp Acerola Powder
0.5 Tbsp Infant Probiotic Blend (Natren Life Start)
0.5 Tbsp Molasses, MCT Oil, or BlueGreen Algae Powder if baby is constipated*

Optional ingredients can add more calories, but are not needed if baby is at ideal weight

NOURISHED IS BEST

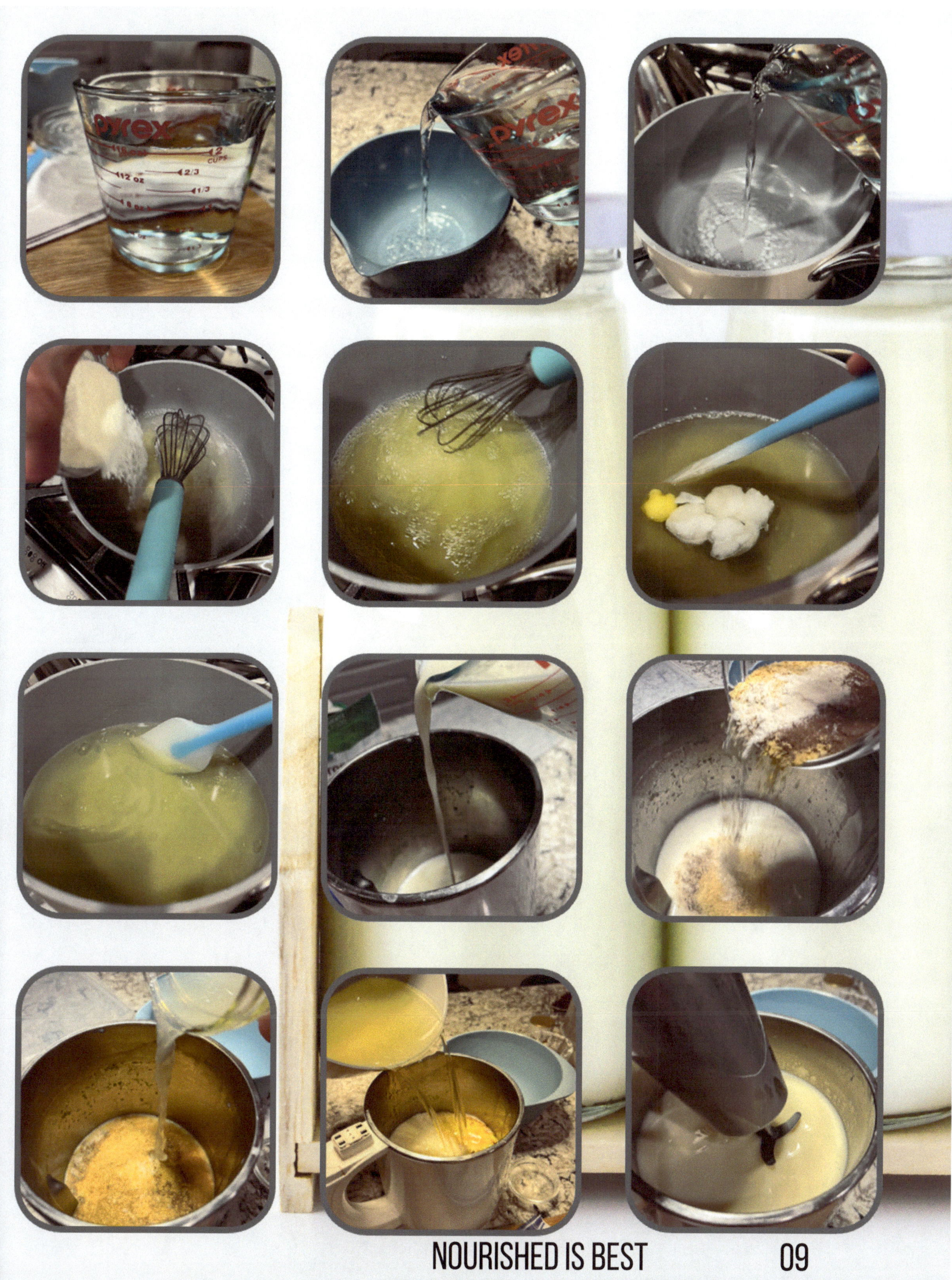

Steps To Prepare

RAW MILK BABY FORMULA
NEWBORN TO 6-9 MONTHS

1. Fill a bowl with 2 cups cold water and set aside. Fill a pan with 2 cups of room temperature water on stove; set to medium-low.

2. Add gelatin and lactose and let dissolve, stir occasionally.

3. Remove from heat and add the cool water; set aside (adding hot ingredients to the milk will accidentally pasteurize the formula).

4. Stir in coconut oil and butter oil until melted.

5. Put the remaining ingredients in a glass blender, or I recommend using a Soya Power G5 blender, as you can also use it for nut milk, soups, etc.

6. Add water/gelatin/lactose mixture to a blender and blend for 5-10 seconds.

7. Place formula in glass baby bottle jars with lids and refrigerate.

8. Milk can be given warm if the baby prefers. However, our children preferred it cold, which also helped with teething.

Nourishes, Looks, Freezes, Thaws, & Even Tastes Like Breast Milk!

Raw Milk Toddler Green Nutrient Drink

6-9 MONTHS TO TODDLER AGE

PREP TIME: 10 MIN
TOTAL TIME: 10 MIN
SERVINGS: APPROX. 80 OZ.

4 Cups Raw Animal Milk of Choice
4 Cups Filtered Mineral Water
1 Tbsp Cod Liver Oil
2 Tbsp Sunflower Oil
2 Tbsp Extra Virgin Olive Oil
4 Tbsp Nutritional Yeast (optional)*
0.5 Tbsp Acerola Powder (optional)*
0.5 Tbsp Infant Probiotic Blend (Natren Life Start)
0.5 Tbsp BlueGreen Algae Powder (Raw Organic)

Optional ingredients can add more calories, but are not needed if baby is at ideal weight

Steps To Prepare

1. This version is much quicker, as the gelatin or oils do not require heating on the stove. I occasionally add nutritional yeast and acerola powder to some versions for extra nutrients when needed. I don't add to every batch unless extra carbs/calories are needed. Add all ingredients into a glass blender, or I recommend using a Soya Power G5 blender, as you can also use it for nut milk, soups, etc. Blend for 5- 10 seconds.

2.   Place formula in glass baby bottle jars with lids and refrigerate. Milk can be given warm if the baby prefers. However, our children preferred it cold, which also helped with teething (two year molars!)

Raw Milk Chocolate Nutrient Drink

KIDS & ADULTS OF ALL AGES

PREP TIME: 10 MIN
TOTAL TIME: 10 MIN
SERVINGS: APPROX. 80 OZ.

4 Cups Raw Animal Milk of Choice
4 Cups Filtered Mineral Water
1/4 Cup Organic Chocolate Syrup (or Raw Agave mixed with Raw Cacao)
4 Tbsp Nutritional Yeast (optional)*
0.5 Tbsp Acerola Powder (optional)*
1 Tbsp Liquid Whey (Raw, Organic) (optional)*
0.5 Tbsp BlueGreen Algae Powder (Raw, Organic)*

*Optional ingredients can add more calories or nutrients, but are not needed for taste

Steps To Prepare

1. This version is much quicker, as the gelatin or oils do not require heating on the stove. I occasionally add nutritional yeast and acerola powder to some versions for extra nutrients when needed. More or less chocolate can be used if desired; liquid whey can also used in this variation. Add all ingredients into a glass blender, or I recommend using a Soya Power G5 blender, as you can also use it for nut milk, soups, etc. Blend for 5-10 seconds.

2. Place in a desired glass jar with a lid and refrigerate. Kids of all ages can drink this, and adults as well. This is also wonderful as a post-workout recovery drink/postpartum drink.

Raw Milk Baby Formula Plant Based

NEWBORN TO 6-9 MONTHS

PREP TIME: 10 MIN
TOTAL TIME: 20 MIN
SERVINGS: APPROX. 80 OZ.

4 Cups Raw Plant Milk of Choice
4 Cups Filtered Mineral Water
8 Tbsp Lactose
4 Tbsp Raw or Pasteurized Cream (optional)*
1 Tbsp Liquid Whey (Raw, Organic) (optional)*
1 Tbsp Cod Liver Oil
2 Tbsp Sunflower Oil
2 Tbsp Extra Virgin Olive Oil
4 Tbsp Virgin Coconut Oil
4 Tbsp Nutritional Yeast
4 Tbsp Gelatin
0.5 Tbsp Acerola Powder
0.5 Tbsp Infant Probiotic Blend (Natren Life Start)
0.5 Tbsp Molasses, MCT Oil, or BlueGreen Algae Powder if baby is constipated*

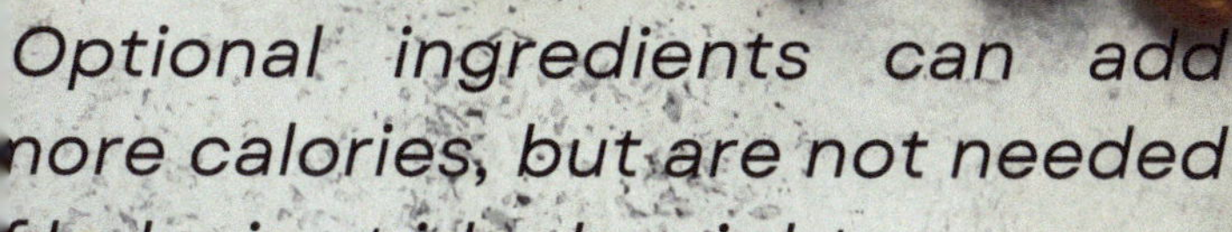

Optional ingredients can add more calories, but are not needed if baby is at ideal weight

NOURISHED IS BEST

17

Steps To Prepare

RAW MILK BABY FORMULA PLANT BASED
NEWBORN TO 6-9 MONTHS

1. Fill a bowl with 2 cups cold water and set aside. Fill a pan with 2 cups of room temperature water on stove; set to medium-low.

2. Add gelatin and lactose and let dissolve, stir occasionally.

3. Remove from heat and add the cool water; set aside (adding hot ingredients to the milk will accidentally pasteurize the formula).

4. Stir in coconut oil until melted.

5. Put the remaining ingredients in a glass blender, or I recommend using a Soya Power G5 blender, as you can also use it for soups and to create the nut milk for this formula (making your own nut milk is highly recommended, as water quality can be controlled and the nuts are sure to be raw and pure.)

6. Add water/gelatin/lactose mixture to a blender and blend for 5-10 seconds.

7. Place formula in glass baby bottle jars with lids and refrigerate.

8. Milk can be given warm if the baby prefers. However, our children preferred it cold, which also helped with teething.

INGREDIENTS

Radiant Life has a formula kit that has all trustworthy, organic brands.

Do not use high-oleic sunflower oil. Use only the brand recommended in the ingredients list: cold pressed, organic, unrefined, and low oleic.

Using high-quality water is imperative to create a healthy formula. Water structure (molecular structure) is the difference between holy/healing water and bulk/dead water...this is important for both making your own formula and plant-based milk (anything water is used for, if living water is used, it can be a remedy). My favorite book explaining this topic is called Water Codes: The Science of Health, Consciousness, and Enlightenment by Carly Nuday, Ph.D.

Do not substitute pasteurized or powdered milk, as these are heavily processed, denatured and allergenic foods. However, pasteurized can be used in an emergency and would be superior to commercial formulas if needed.

Do not use ultra-pasteurized (UHT) cream. It is highly allergenic. Raw or pasteurized cream is best.

Do not use fish or krill oil instead of high vitamin cod liver oil (does not contain Vitamin D or very little VitaminA). Unflavored is also fine.

Collagen powder can be substituted for gelatin if needed. Powder whey (1 tsp) and 1/2 cup water can be combined instead of liquid whey.

FYI, raw milk contains the necessary iron needed for this formula.

Tips

RATIOS

Ingredient	Amount Required per Batch	Number of Batches per Container
Infant Bifidum - (2.5 oz)	1/4 Tsp	140
Acerola Powder - (6 oz)	1/4 Tsp	188
Lactose - (4-1 lb bags)	8 Tbsp	19
Coconut Oil - (16 oz)	4 Tbsp	24
Gelatin - (14 oz)	4 Tbsp	30
Sunflower Oil - (8.5 oz)	2 Tbsp	25
Nutritional Yeast - (1 lb)	4 Tbsp	52
Olive Oil - (1/2 Liter)	2 Tbsp	49
Cod Liver Oil - (6.1 oz)	1 Tbsp	45
Butter Oil (6.1 oz)	1/4 Tsp	192

As if you pumped it yourself!

Tips

FAVORITE BRAND INGREDIENTS & RAW MILK INFO

- NOW (Lactose and Acerola Powder)
- Bariani (Olive Oil)
- Radiant Life (Coconut Oil)
- Flora (Sunflower Oil)
- Bernard Jensen's (Gelatin)
- Rosita (Cod Liver Oil)
- Frontier Co-op (Nutritional Yeast)
- Grass-Fed High-Vitamin Butter Oil
- Bluegreen Algae from Klamath Lake Oregon
- True Spring Water Solutions (Energized and Filtered Structured Water)
- Holy water from Lourdes (a few drops change the molecular structure of the whole batch!)

The benefits of raw milk are well documented when the animals are treated and fed well, and proper tests are done for bacteria. 'Germ Theory' was created and subsequently, fears spread against the use of raw milk, however many families swear by the results; there is no other 'liquid gold' than this.

Tips

RAW MILK INFO CONTINUED

UNITED STATES

RAW MILK IS AVAILABLE BY STATE LEVEL IN THE UNITED STATES — SOME ALLOW SALES IN STORES AND SOME ALLOW SOMETHING CALLED A RAW MILK HERD SHARE (WHEREYOU BUY INTO A HERD AND OWN THE COW, THEN ARE ABLE TO GET YOUR OWN MILK). RAW MILK IS LEGAL IN 12 STATES FOR RETAIL SALES, 15 STATES FOR ON-FARM SALES, AND 4 STATES FOR HERDSHARES. IN ARIZONA, UTAH, CALIFORNIA, AND WASHINGTON, RAW MILK CAN BE SOLD IN RETAIL STORES WITH APPROPRIATE WARNING LABELS.

UNITED KINGDOM

RAW MILK IS LEGAL IN ENGLAND, WALES, AND NORTHERN IRELAND, BUT IT CAN ONLY BE SOLD DIRECTLY TO THE CONSUMER BY REGISTERED MILK PRODUCTION FARMS OR AT REGISTERED FARMERS' MARKETS.

NEW ZEALAND

CERTIFIED RAW MILK IS AVAILABLE DIRECTLY FROM DAIRY FARMS, INCLUDING VENDING MACHINES.

OTHER EUROPEAN COUNTRIES

RAW MILK IS LEGAL IN MANY EUROPEAN COUNTRIES, INCLUDING FRANCE, ITALY, AND SWITZERLAND.

MIDDLE/SOUTH AMERICA

RAW MILK LEGALITY IN SOUTH AMERICA VARIES BY COUNTRY AND REGION, WITH SOME COUNTRIES ALLOWING THE PRODUCTION AND SALE OF RAW MILK, WHILE OTHERS PROHIBIT IT. RAW MILK PRODUCTS ARE AVAILABLE IN MEXICO.

MIDDLE EAST

IN THE MIDDLE EAST, RAW MILK IS LEGAL IN SOME AREAS, BUT ILLEGAL IN OTHERS DUE TO HYGIENE CONCERNS.

ASIA

RAW MILK IS LEGAL FOR SALE IN INDIA. RAW MILK IS LEGAL IN MOST ASIAN COUNTRIES, WHERE LAWS PROHIBITING IT ARE EITHER NONEXISTENT OR RARELY ENFORCED. HOWEVER, THE REGULATIONS FOR RAW MILK VARY BY COUNTRY.

CANADA

RAW MILK IS NOT LEGAL IN CANADA.

Tips

- A BLENDER CAN BE USED. HOWEVER, A SOYA POWER G5 IS WORTH THE INVESTMENT AND CAN BE USED TO MAKE OTHER HOME GOODS (NUT MILK, SOUPS, FRESH JUICE, ETC). THERE ARE SEVERAL HOT SETTINGS, SO MAKE SURE TO USE THE 'RAW/JUICE' SETTING.

- AVENT, OR ANY OTHER 8 OZ. GLASS BOTTLES CAN BE USED; THIS RECIPE MAKES ABOUT 8 BOTTLES (FULL).

- I USED COSMETIC FRIDGES BY THE BED, BUT THESE ARE RAW MILK-BASED AND CAN SIT OUT ALL NIGHT WITHOUT BECOMING HARMFUL. MY CHILDREN TOOK THE BOTTLES COLD, WHICH ALSO HELPED WITH TEETHING, AND CUT OUT A STEP FOR ME — I RECOMMEND YOU TRY WHAT WORKS FOR YOUR LITTLE ONES. UNFINISHED BOTTLES CAN BE SAVED AND USED AGAIN. SIMPLY REFRIGERATE.

- I USE TWO BINS TO KEEP ALL INGREDIENTS, SO I CAN GRAB THEM OUT QUICKLY (ANYTHING TO KEEP YOU FROM GETTING OVERWHELMED) — ONCE YOU MAKE IT A FEW TIMES, YOU'RE ALREADY AN EXPERT!

- ESSENTIAL PREP ITEMS: RUBBER SPATULA, MIXING BOWL WITH A SPOUT(TO POUR INTO GLASS BOTTLES, UNLESS USING A BLENDER WITH SPOUT), SMALL POT, MEASURING SPOONS/CUP, AND I LIKE TO USE LITTLE PREP BOWLS TO COMBINE THE GELATIN/LACTOSE, AND ANOTHER FOR THE ACEROLA POWDER/PROBIOTIC POWDER/NUTRITIONAL YEAST, AND A THIRD BOWL FOR BUTTER OIL AND COCONUT OIL. THIS MAKES IT QUICK TO THROW THE INGREDIENTS TOGETHER WHEN NEEDED.

The Raw Milkmaid® City Homesteader Series

Make sure to check out other books by the Author:
Leftovers to Luxury, a scrappy leftovers cookbook, and three more cookbooks on the way in the next twelve months.

Also see her children's series, The Power of the Rose, and her poetry, Love: Through the Looking Glass.

About the Author

CATHERINE DEVINE ZAGORSKI

Catherine Devine Zagorski foundedVeda Ventures MalkootaD'Shmeya – a company dedicated to the will of the rising Divine Feminine, formed duringthe blood, sweat,and tears of new motherhood. She is ditching her corporate executive title for the identity she has always known as inside The Water Priestess. She is now on a mission to heal and mother herself and her children and to nurture a dark and hurting world...a humanity hungry for the origins of their celestial beginnings and the end to their attachment to suffering.

After a harrowing journey with recurrent miscarriages and infertility having the full support of her husband to have 'wild pregnancies' and two miracle home birthsat the age of 39 and 40, she was brought to her true calling: helping women to see the divine creator within them, and bringing the fear out of conception, pregnancy, birth, breastfeeding, and parenting in general. Once the baby arrives,a new set of complications arise, and each family's feeding journey is different. Still, there is usually one commontheme used to make sure most moms supplement with commercial formula... the same stigma surrounding the birth itself...and that is fear. Fear is the opposite of LOVE (our natural state). It is the mission of this author to welcome the authentic Nature of each human and how we were born and fed in the days of old....toeliminate the fear and bring back the sacredness and wonder of birth and early childhood...to empower and support the ability of each parentto confidently becomethe new transformed version of themselves – the personthei baby came to meet. This authoris convinced that NOW is the time humanity takes back the holy Nature of birth...and of feedingourselves with Nature's goodness - straight from the farm, made with love by Mama This is the time to guard future generations' sanctity and honor our ancestors.

From the Author

CATHERINE DEVINE ZAGORSKI

wasn't until I became a mother that I realized how hard it was to remain in the corporate world and be taken seriously. To try to go back to a semblance of my 'old self' and even take myself seriously. I also realized how hard it is for stay-at-home moms with little to no support or sleep and husbands stressed over work and financial obligations. It is hard for working mothers to manage to keep a job, much less to breastfeed their kids while maintaining this focus, or even just recovering from birth, and pregnancy alone is hard on the body before the strain of generating milk. How hard it must be for adoptive parents having no access to donor breast milk, or C-section and other moms with delays on milk coming in; or mothers like me who had a low milk supply and would need to supplement with formula. Having only the option of breastfeeding (probably the healthiest food in the world!) or the equivalent of dry powdered milk that most of us wouldn't drink ourselves? How are THESE the only two options...either the best food from our bodies or the worst chemically laced food from a can? Where is the middle ground?

A journey that began with a stress-based low milk supply, only to realize the myriad of issues women (and all parents) face around the basic, yes BASIC, idea of feeding their children – has led to the birth of this nourishing and homemade 'just like breast milk 'baby formula. From that, it blossomed into a 'toddler' green drink' and a big-kid/teen/adult chocolate nutrient drink (great for post-workout recovery!), as the postpartum period truly taught me how much my body needed these nutrients, not just my child. My husband also needed the nutrients after becoming a father, and our whole family has benefited exponentially from this beautiful and ancient cow's milk. The strain around this topic is not discussed enough, and the support is lacking – almost more than the options for a healthy, living, nourishing formula...something as healthy as breast milk. Still, it allows the mother to recover without guilt...which didn't seem to exist UNTIL NOW!

plan to take the discrimination and retaliation I faced in the corporate workplace and turn it into something beautiful. An empire is dedicated to the family, the mothers, the caretakers, and those who do the silent work that is often unnoticed and undervalued. The ones changing the world with the love in their hearts; the ones who are Mothering us back to health, ushering in the New Earth, and leading the return of humanity to its rightful place: as ONE, in harmony with nature and each other.

www.ingramcontent.com/pod-product-compliance
Lightning Source LLC
Chambersburg PA
CBHW042128110726
48006CB00003B/808